KAYE WEBB was greatly loved and respected for her contribution to the children's book world. As publishing director of the children's division of Penguin, she was one of the first female directors in British publishing.

She was founder of the Puffin Club, which put her in direct contact with the tastes and interests of children all over the country, and she was a prolific editor and anthologist. Her death in 1996 was a sad loss to young readers everywhere.

"Birthday Treat" – text © Ian Seraillier 1992, illustrations © Quentin Blake 1992;
"Baldilocks and the Six Bears" – text © Dick King-Smith 1992, illustrations © Clive Scruton 1992;
"Sensible Food" – text © Christopher Fry 1992, illustrations © Russell Ayto 1992;
"The Sandboat" – text © Berlie Doherty 1992, illustrations © Joanna Burroughes 1992;
"Sea Poems" – text © Ted Hughes 1992, illustration © Pauline Baynes 1992;
"Secrets" – text © Betsy Byars 1992, illustrations © Catherine Brighton 1992;
"Bridesmaid" – text © Mick Gowar 1992, illustrations © Priscilla Lamont 1992;
"Page Twenty-three" – text © Michael Rosen 1992, illustrations © Tony Ross 1992;
"Days" – text © Charles Causley 1992, illustrations © Jan Pienkowski 1992;
"The Birthday Cake" – text © Margaret Mahy 1992, illustrations © Margaret Chamberlain 1992;
"Jamie" – text © Sheila Lavelle 1992, illustrations © Emma Chichester Clark 1992.
Cover illustration © Margaret Chamberlain 1992.

First published in Great Britain in 1992 by
Frances Lincoln Children's Books, 4 Torriano Mews,
Torriano Avenue, London NW5 2RZ
www.franceslincoln.com

This paperback edition published in 2007

British Library Cataloguing in Publication Data available on request

ISBN 978-1-84507-712-9

Printed in China

1 3 5 7 9 8 6 4 2

Round About Six

Stories and Poems by your
Favourite Writers and Illustrators

Chosen by Kaye Webb

F

FRANCES LINCOLN
CHILDREN'S BOOKS

Contents

Birthday Treat

IAN SERRAILLIER

After a birthday tea

    they staggered out to see

        the pond

           and beyond.

              Matthew (six today)

                led the way.

William spent some time
stirring the slime.

Edward caught a newt
in his Wellington boot.

Simon squashed a snail
under his pail.

He meant no harm, but Dominic
was sick.

Baldilocks and the Six Bears

DICK KING-SMITH

There was once a magic forest full of fine tall trees.

In it lived not only animals, but – because it was a magic forest – fairies and pixies and elves and goblins. Some of the goblins were full of mischief and some of the elves were rather spiteful, but on the whole, the fairy people were a happy lot. All except for one.

He was a hobgoblin, quite young, not bad-looking; he might even have been thought handsome except for one thing.

He hadn't a hair on his head.

Some one – probably an elf – had named him Baldilocks, and that was what everyone called him.

Baldilocks had never had a great deal of hair, and what he did have had gradually fallen out, till now he had none at all.

How sad he was. How he envied all the other fairy people their fine locks and tresses, each time they met, at the full moon.

In a clearing among the trees was a huge fairy-ring, and in the middle of this ring sat the wisest fairy of them all. She was known as the Queen of the Forest.

As usual, everyone laughed when Baldilocks came into the fairy-ring.

"Baldilocks!" someone – probably an elf – would shout, and then the pixies would titter and the elves would snigger and the goblins would chuckle and the fairies would giggle. All except for one.

She was a little red-haired fairy, not specially beautiful but with such a kindly face. She alone did not laugh at the bald hobgoblin.

One moonlit night, when everyone was teasing poor Baldilocks as usual, the Queen of the Forest called for silence. Then she said to Baldilocks, "Would you like to grow a fine head of hair?"

"Oh I would, Your Majesty!" cried the hobgoblin. "But how do I go about it?"

"Ask a bear," said the Queen of the Forest, and not a word more would she say.

The very next morning Baldilocks set out to find a bear. It did not take him long.

He came to a muddy pool, and there was a big brown bear, catching frogs.

"Excuse me," said Baldilocks. "Could you tell me how to grow a fine head of hair?"

The brown bear looked carefully at the hobgoblin. He knew that the only way a bald person can grow hair is by rubbing bear's grease into his scalp. But he wasn't going to say that, because he knew that the only way to get bear's grease is to kill a bear and melt him down.

He picked up a pawful of mud.

"Rub this into your scalp," said the brown bear.

So Baldilocks took the sticky mud and rubbed it on his head. It was full of wriggling things and it smelt horrid. But it didn't make one single hair grow.

The next bear Baldilocks met was a big black one. It was robbing a wild bees' nest.

"Excuse me," said Baldilocks. "Could you tell me how to grow a fine head of hair?"

The black bear looked carefully at the hobgoblin. He too knew the only way for a bald person to grow hair. He pulled out a pawful of honeycomb.

"Rub this into your scalp," said the black bear.

So Baldilocks took the honey and rubbed it on his head. It was horribly sticky and it had several angry bees in it that stung him. But it didn't make one single hair grow.

The third bear that Baldilocks met was a big gingery one, that was digging for grubs in a nettle patch.

Baldilocks asked his question again, and the ginger bear, after looking carefully at him, pulled up a pawful of nettles and said, "Rub these into your scalp."

So Baldilocks took the nettles and rubbed them on his head. They stung him so much that his eyes began to water, but they didn't make one single hair grow.

The fourth bear that Baldilocks came across, a big chocolate-coloured one, was digging out an ants' nest, and by way of reply to the hobgoblin, he handed him a pawful of earth that was full of ants.

When Baldilocks rubbed it on his head, the ants bit him so hard that the tears rolled down his face, but they didn't make one single hair grow. Baldilocks found the fifth bear by the side of a river that ran through the forest. It was a big old grey bear, and it was eating some fish that had been left high and dry on the bank by a flood. They seemed to have been dead for a long time, and when Baldilocks' question had been asked and answered, and he had rubbed the rotten fish on his head, they made it smell perfectly awful. But, once again, they didn't make one single hair grow.

Baldilocks had just about had enough. What with the mud and the honey and all the stings and bites and the stink of the fish, he almost began to hope that he wouldn't meet another bear. But he did.

It was a baby bear, a little golden one, and it was sitting in the sun doing nothing.

"Excuse me," said Baldilocks. "Could you tell me how to grow a fine head of hair?"

The baby bear looked fearfully at the hobgoblin. He knew, although he was so young, that the only way for a bald person to grow hair is by rubbing bear's grease into his scalp. And he knew, although he was so young, that the only way to get bear's grease is to kill a bear and melt him down.

He did not answer, so Baldilocks, to encourage him, said, "I expect you'll tell me to rub something into my scalp."

"Yes," said the baby bear in a small voice.

"What?"

"Bear's grease," said the baby bear in a very small voice.

"Bear's grease?" said Baldilocks. "How do I get hold of that?"

"You have to kill a bear," said the baby bear in a whisper, "and melt him down."

"Oh!" said Baldilocks. "Oh no!" he said.

When next the fairy people met, and the hobgoblin came into the fairy-ring, someone – probably an elf – shouted "Baldilocks!" and everyone laughed, except the little red-haired fairy.

The Queen of the Forest called for silence. Then she said to Baldilocks, "You haven't grown any hair. Didn't you ask a bear?"

"I asked six, Your Majesty," said Baldilocks, "before I found out that what I need is bear's grease, and to get that I would have to kill a bear and melt him down."

"That might be difficult," said the Queen of the Forest, "but perhaps you could kill a little one?"

She smiled as she spoke, because she knew, being the wisest fairy of them all, that high in a nearby tree a small golden bear sat listening anxiously.

"I couldn't do such a thing," said Baldilocks. "I'd sooner stay bald and unhappy."

Up in the tree, the baby bear hugged himself, silently.

After the others had gone away, Baldilocks still sat alone in the fairy-ring. At least he thought he was alone, till he looked round and saw that the little red-haired fairy with the kindly face was still sitting there too.

"I think," she said, "that bald people are much the nicest."

"You do?" said Baldilocks.

"Yes. So you mustn't be unhappy any more. If you are, you will make me very sad."

Baldilocks looked at her, and to his eyes it seemed that she didn't simply have a kindly face, she was beautiful.

He smiled the happiest of smiles.

"You mustn't be sad," he said. "That's something I couldn't bear."

Sensible Food

CHRISTOPHER FRY

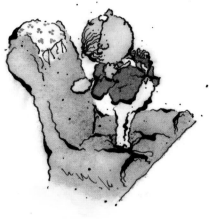

Crispin Crunch
Had porridge for lunch
And stew for breakfast and tea.
As he sensibly said:
This is not how you're fed
As a *rule* in the Land of the Free.

Crispin Crunch
Took a tentative munch
(Though a muncher of porridge is rare).
Then he found to his shame
That a blob of the same
Had managed to get in his hair.

Crispin Crunch
Had a positive hunch
That this was unusual for food.
So he rang a big bell
And remarked "It's as well
That I'm in an uncritical mood."

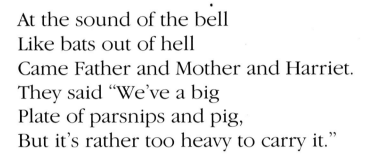

At the sound of the bell
Like bats out of hell
Came Father and Mother and Harriet.
They said "We've a big
Plate of parsnips and pig,
But it's rather too heavy to carry it."

Crispin Crunch
Had a *sensible* lunch
Of –––––– and –––––– and cheese.
He received it with thanks.
You can fill in the blanks
With whatever you jolly well please.

The Sandboat

BERLIE DOHERTY

Joe filled two buckets with wet sand and carried them up to where his mum and dad were sitting in their stripy deckchairs.

"Cover your arms up, Joe," his mum said. "Don't you go and get sunburnt." She was shiny with sun-tan oil, like a big pink dolphin.

"Don't wander off," his dad said, "or you'll get lost." He took his shoes and socks off and wiggled his toes about like crabs in the sand.

Joe fetched some more wet sand and tipped it out of the buckets.

"Don't tip that sand out near me," Mum said. "It'll get in my eyes."

Dad said: "Don't get it in your hair, Joe, or we'll have to bath you tonight."

Joe fetched more sand and tipped it out.

"Don't bring any more of that wet sand over here," his mum said.

"You've got enough," said Dad.

"Leave some for other people," his mum said.

Joe stood up. The tide was coming in, like a long

brown snuffling creature. He ran down with his buckets and filled them up again. He stood by his pile and dolloped the new sand down.

"Stop chucking sand about," his mum said. She closed her eyes and yawned.

Joe picked up his red spade and dug a hollow in the middle of his sand pile. He patted the sides.

"Don't get your hands muddy," Dad said, half asleep.

Joe dug and dug and built and built. He wasn't sure what he was making, except that it had a rounded front and a hollow inside with a little built-up bit like a seat, and it was long. The sun grew high and hot. The sea snuffled nearer and nearer.

"Don't get wet," Mum murmured, and fell fast asleep.

Dad snored. "Don't . . ." he rumbled.

All of a sudden Joe knew what he was building. It was a boat. It was definitely a boat. He was excited now. He ran from side to side and all round it, adding a bit more sand, patting the sides, rubbing them to make them round. It was a beautiful boat. He stuck a long white gull's feather on the front bit, the prow. He lay flat on his belly and blew the feather and it fluttered, just like a flag.

He stuck shells along the sides in a long line. Then he stood up. The brown snuffly tide was almost in. He climbed into his sandboat and sat on the seat that was only just big enough for him, and waited.

Slowly the sea crept round the boat. Joe watched the water trickle as far as Dad's bare toes, but it didn't wake him up. It dribbled round Mum's bag of sandwiches, but it didn't wake her up. Joe wriggled in his sandy seat. The sea was all round him.

And then Joe's boat began to move. At first it was just a little rocking movement, and then it seemed to lift and sway like a swing, gently up, gently down, and then it was floating. It was really floating. The white feather fluttered like a real flag.

Joe sailed past the men and women and dogs who were paddling round him. He sailed past the children who were jumping up and down and splashing and shrieking. He sailed past the bobbing heads of all the swimmers, past them, past them all, out to sea. He trailed his hands over the edge and felt the waves slapping his fingers. He could feel the spray tickling his cheeks. He laughed out loud, and high above him the seagulls laughed too.

He looked over his shoulder and saw, far behind him, the tiny figures on the beach. He could just see Mum and Dad, fast asleep in their deckchairs.

Shoals of fishes drifted round him, flashing like stars in the water. The waves sparkled in the sunlight. When

he closed his eyes he could hear the whales singing to each other, miles and miles below him. He sang back to them, as loud as he could, at the top of his voice, louder than he'd ever sung in his life before. A dolphin jumped out of the water and clapped its fins at him.

Far away he could see a huge ship, like a castle in the water. It was an ocean liner. It loomed up to him, rocking his little sandboat with the giant white waves it made. His dolphin leapt in the air with excitement. Booom! went the ship's loud hooter. "Tooot!" shouted Joe. "Toooot!" The captain came on deck and saluted him. Joe stood up in his sandboat and saluted back.

"That's a fine craft you have, Captain!" the captain shouted.

"Thank you, Captain," shouted Joe. He felt as round as an egg with pride.

"Going far?" the captain shouted.

"Miles!" Joe shouted back. "Are you going far?"

"Australia!" said the captain.

"Don't get lost!" Joe shouted, and he and the captain laughed.

"I might!" said the captain. "It's a long way to Australia!"

"You can borrow my dolphin if you like," said Joe, and his dolphin flicked its tail and swam off towards the liner, to lead it all the way to Australia.

Joe waved to the liner till it was out of sight. He looked over the side of his boat, and saw the fishes swimming like seagulls in the water. He looked up and saw the seagulls floating like fishes in the sky.

All of a sudden his boat gave a little soft bump, and Joe realised that he had landed on the shore. The tide was trickling away from him, like a long snuffling creature scurrying back home. It whispered away like smoke. Joe climbed out of his boat. It was strange to be standing still again, on dry land.

Mum and Dad were just beginning to wake up.

"I hope you didn't wander off," said Dad.

"I hope you haven't eaten the sandwiches," said Mum. She looked in her bag. "Just look at them. They're wet!"

"Why didn't you tell us the tide was coming in?" said Dad.

"We could have floated away on our deckchairs," said Mum.

And Joe smiled to himself, and didn't say a word.

Sea Poems

TED HUGHES

Limpet

When Surf slams
His tower so hard
The Lighthouse-keeper's
Teeth are jarred

The Limpet laughs
Beneath her hat:
"There's nothing I love
So much as that!

Great seas of shock
That roar to knock me
Off my rocker
Rock me, rock me."

Mussel

When you prise
Her shells apart
To say Hello
The Mussel cries:
"I know! I know!
I confess
I am a mess.
But I'm all heart –
Heart that could not
Softer soften!

An ugly girl,
But often, often
With a pearl."

29

Secrets

BETSY BYARS

Jimmy had never kept a secret in his life. Nobody would even tell him one any more. So far this year he had already told three.

The first secret was that his sister was getting a kitten for her birthday. He ran up the stairs so fast to tell her that he missed the last step. He fell flat on his face.

He jumped up. He threw open her door. He said, "Guess what you're getting for your birthday?" Before she could guess, he yelled, "A kitten!"

To his surprise his sister was not pleased. She even got mad. She yelled, "Mum! Jimmy told me what I'm getting. Now it won't be a surprise!"

When she got the kitten, the first thing she said to it was, "You were supposed to be a surprise, but Big Mouth told."

At Christmas he got another chance. "We're getting Mum new dishes," his sister said. "Now, don't tell!"

"I won't."

He ran into the kitchen. "I know what you're getting for Christmas."

"Don't tell," his mother said. "I like to be surprised."

"I won't tell." Then he couldn't help himself. He added, "But they're round and you eat off them."

"Jimmy!" his sister yelled.

When his mother opened the dishes, she said, "They are just beautiful."

His sister said, "But Big Mouth ruined the surprise."

It was like that all the time. He didn't want to tell. He just couldn't help himself.

At school he had ruined the birthday surprise party for Miss Brown. Miss Brown was called to the office, and while she was gone, one of the mothers had brought in a large box and hid it in the back of the room. When the teacher came in, Jimmy said, "Miss Brown! Miss Brown!"

"Yes, Jimmy."

"Someone left a box in the back of the room."

"Thank you, Jimmy, now get out your reading books."

"Miss Brown! Miss Brown!"

"Yes, Jimmy."

"It's a cake!"

 No one would speak to Jimmy. At break one boy even hit him. "You told," he said. "You ruined the whole party." Jimmy dusted himself off and hung his head. He wished he had not told, but he couldn't help himself.

After that Jimmy was afraid no one would ever tell him a secret again. And he knew too that there was a secret going around his class room. Just that morning when he came in, all the other kids stopped talking.

"What's up?" he asked his friend Roman.

Roman shrugged.

"Is it something I should know about?"

Roman said, "No."

That night Jimmy told his sister, "Everybody in my room knows a secret and they won't tell me."

"I don't blame them," said his sister.

"Why?"

"Because you blab. I know two secrets, and you would be the last person in the world I would tell."

"You know two secrets?"

"Yes."

"What are they?"

"No!"

"Just tell me one."

His sister left the room.

The next morning when Jimmy went to school he stopped outside the door. He listened. He heard someone say, "Shhhh! He's outside. He's listening. Don't give it away."

Everything got very quiet. Jimmy walked into the room and sat at his desk. In a low voice he said, "Please tell me the secret, Roman."

"No."

"I'd tell you."

"I know you would."

"Pleasssssssse!"

"Nnnnnooooooooo."

"Then I'll find out from somebody else."

After school he waited at the corner for Libby Rose. In Class One Libby had had trouble keeping a secret too. She had told that Rickie had a little snake in his pocket. Well, she had not actually told. She had said, "Mr Rogers, is it all right for us to bring snakes to school in our pockets?"

When he saw Libby, he said, "Libby, what's the big secret?"

Libby said, "I'm not telling."

"If I ever hear a secret, I'm not going to tell you."

"You're never going to hear one."

He followed Libby down the sidewalk on his knees. "Please please please please –"

"Oh, all right," Libby said. "Our teacher's going to get married."

He got up and dusted off his knees. He ran home like a cartoon character, leaving a streak behind him. He flung open the door. "I found out the secret! Our teacher's going to get married."

"She's already married," his mother said. "Somebody's teasing you."

That night he tried a desperate trick. He phoned Roman. "Well, I heard the big secret."

Roman said, "Did you?"

"Yes, so I guess it's no secret any more."

"I guess not."

"So we can talk about it, right?"

"Right. Who told you?"

Jimmy said, "First you tell me the secret so I can see if it's the same secret. Then I'll tell who told."

Roman said, "No deal."

"Just tell me one of the words in the secret."

But Roman hung up.

It was worse the next day. Jimmy was late for school. He could hear the class buzzing all the way down the corridor. He burst into the room. Silence. He decided to try another trick.

He said, "I heard you! I've been outside listening the whole time."

"Prove it," said Libby. "What did you hear?"

Jimmy stood there for a minute. Then he said, "Oh, nothing," and he went to his seat.

It was the longest secret in the world. It went on and on. Day after day, Jimmy would guess, "It's a party for somebody!" or, "The whole class is going to the zoo!"

or, "We're going to give a play!" But he could tell from how happy his friends looked that he had not guessed right.

Finally Jimmy got tired of begging. When he came into the room on Monday and everyone was whispering, he just went to his seat. When he came into the room on Tuesday

and they were whispering louder, he just went to his seat.

On Wednesday, only two girls were whispering. Jimmy went to his seat. On Thursday, no one was whispering at all. Jimmy was glad about that. He went to his seat.

On Friday after school Roman surprised Jimmy. Roman said, "You want to know what the secret was?"

"Not any more," Jimmy said. "I've lost interest in secrets."

Roman said, "Then I'll tell you. The secret was that there was no secret."

"What?"

"The secret was that there was no secret. We just made you think there was one."

"There wasn't any secret?"

"There *was* a secret," Roman explained. "It was that there was no secret!"

"I *hate* that secret!"

"We knew you would."

"It's the worst secret I ever heard in my life! I hate that secret. Who thought of that terrible secret?"

"Everybody."

"Well, I hate it. I just hate it!"

"I do too," Roman said.

They started walking home. At the corner, Jimmy said, "You know, I think I'm cured."

Roman said, "What?"

"It's like having measles. You get over it, and you don't ever have it again. I had a bad case of secrets. Now I'm cured."

And his friend Roman said, "That's good."

Bridesmaid

MICK GOWAR

On the hanger on my bedroom door
is a dress like a princess's.

If I was seven or eight or nine
or ten I'd be too big,
it wouldn't fit. But I'm six

and six is just right
to wear a dress like a princess's,
with a satin sash
that creaks like crisp snow.

If I was five or four or three
or two or one I'd be too young
to walk up the long aisle of the church
in a dress like a princess's,
with a satin sash
that creaks like crisp snow
and white satin ballet shoes.

But I'm six,
and six is just right
to wear a comb of silk flowers
in my hair,
a dress like a princess's,
a satin sash
that creaks like crisp snow,
white satin ballet shoes,
and walk up the long aisle of the church
carrying a basket of Spring flowers.

Six is exactly right.

Page Twenty-three

MICHAEL ROSEN

It was bedtime. Horrible old bedtime.

Billy was on the top bunk. He was five. Ray was on the bottom bunk. He was nine.

"Are you asleep, Ray?" said Billy.

"No," said Ray. "Are you?"

"Am I what?" said Billy.

"Asleep," said Ray.

"I don't think so," said Billy.

"Neither am I," said Ray.

"I know," said Billy.

"How do you know?" said Ray.

"You just told me," said Billy.

"Did I?" said Ray.

"Yes," said Billy.

"Hey, I've got an idea," said Ray. "Let's get Dad to read us a story."

"Yeah," said Billy.

So they started up the chanting: "Da - a - d. Da - a - d. Da - a - d. Da - a - d."

A voice came from far away: "Shut up will you, you two."

They went on: "Da - a - d. Da - a - d. Da - a - d."

The door burst open. It was Dad. He had egg on his chin and a fork in his hand.

"Dad, you've got egg on your chin," said Ray.

"I'm having my tea. That's why. Don't you want me to have my tea? Can't I have my tea without you two yelling your –"

"You've got a fork in your hand, Dad," said Billy.

"I know I have," said Dad.

"Can you read us a story, Dad?"

"We can't get to sleep."

"And the wall's really boring."

"And we haven't seen you today."

Dad looked a bit less angry. "All right. Now I haven't got long."

"YIPPEEEEEEE!"

Dad grabbed the first book he saw. It was called: *The Great Big Scare Book*. He sat down on a chair next to Ray. Billy leaned over the rail on the top bunk and looked down at them.

Dad began: "In a dark cave where water dripped down the –"

"That one's easy, Dad," said Ray.

"Which one's easy? What do you mean?"

"It's not a real story book, Dad. There are questions on each page and you have to get the answers right."

"This is the book I'm reading to you, OK?" said Dad. "Do you want me to read it or not?"

"OK," said Ray. "Read it. But I know the answer to that one."

"What *is* the answer to this page, then?" said Dad.

"Werewolves' blood," said Ray.

"I see," said Dad. "Well, which one *don't* you know the answer to then, cleverbelly?"

"Page 23," said Ray.

Billy was still looking out over the rail. "Don't turn to page 23, Dad," said Billy. "Don't, please don't."

"Yeah," said Ray. "Turn to page 23."

"No, don't please," said Billy.

Dad turned to page 23. "What's the problem here?"

Dad and Ray looked to see what was written there. Billy stared at the picture. It was a dark creepy slimy picture, with wild things staring out with ugly white eyes and mouldy teeth biting and grinning.

Dad was muttering: "Does the Horror of the Night come through the window when . . ."

He was frowning and holding his head and trying to work it out.

"It's hard, isn't it, Dad?" said Ray.

"Ye - e - s," said Dad. "No, I've got it. The answer is nine."

"Nine what?" said Ray.

"Nine dead worms," said Dad, looking very pleased with himself.

"OK, that's it," he said. He closed the book. "I haven't got any more time."

"Night night, Ray." He kissed Ray and tucked him in.

"Night night, Billy," and he kissed Billy and tucked him in too and off he went.

He sat down to finish his egg. It was cold. He had just got a bit into his mouth when he

heard a strange noise. It was a long thin squealy noise. It sounded terrible.

"Eeeeeeeeeeeeeeeeeeeee!"

It was coming from the boys' bedroom. Dad got up, rushed to their room. There was Billy lying on his back, tears pouring out of his face, his cheeks all crumpled up, his mouth shaking.

"Oh no," thought Dad, "Something's really going wrong here. Maybe he's ill. He'll need a doctor . . . or an ambulance maybe."

"What's the matter, Billy?" he said.

"Page twenty-threeeeeeeeeeeeeeeee," said Billy.

"What about page 23?" said Dad.

"It's the picture. It's scareeeeeeeeeeeeeeeeeeeeee," said Billy.

"The picture can't do you any harm, Billy," said Dad.

"It's coming to get meeeeeeeeeeeeeeeeeeeeeeeee," said Billy.

"Think of something else, Billy. It's not that bad," said Dad.

"Noooooooooooooo. They're coming to get meeeeeeeee."

"Think of something nice. Think of . . . er . . . teddy bears."

"Yeah," said Ray, "and they're coming to get you."

"YAAAAAAAAAAAAAAAAAA!", said Billy.

"Shut up, Ray," said Dad.

Billy was feeling like a very small thing and hundreds of very big things were rushing towards

him. Dad thought he'd sing Billy a funny song. He
sang:

> *"Your Dad is a funny one,*
> *He's got a nose like a pickled onion,*
> *He's got a face like a squashed tomato,*
> *And feet like fried fish."*

Ray said, "Be quiet, Dad. I can't get to sleep."

Billy went on squealing. He was still thinking he was
a very small thing, but now the big things were
roaring about near his ears.

Dad sang two more songs.

Ray said, "Stop singing, Dad. I'm really tired, you
know."

Billy felt as if he was getting smaller and smaller and
smaller.

Dad smacked Billy's pillow to make it more puffy.

Ray said, "Stop banging, Dad," and then he fell
asleep.

Billy was sure he was so small now, he had
disappeared.

"I've gone," he thought. "I've gone."

Dad was thinking about his egg. He sang one more
song:

> *"Here comes Doctor Glannister,*
> *Sliding down the bannister,*
> *Now he's gone and ripped his pants,*
> *Now he's doing a cha-cha dance."*

And Billy fell asleep.

"At last," thought Dad and he crept out of the room and back to the kitchen to finish his egg. It was a very, very cold egg. "Poor old Billy," he thought. "I wonder if he'll still be scared in the morning."

In the morning, Dad and Billy and Ray sat down to have breakfast. Dad was keeping an eye on Billy.

"He doesn't look very well," thought Dad. "He looks terrible."

So Dad said, "Are you all right, Billy?"

"Yep," said Billy.

"You're not scared of anything . . . ?"

"What's there to be scared of?" said Billy.

"I was wondering if you were still worried about the book we looked at last night?"

"Don't be silly, Dad," said Billy. "They're only pictures. Pictures can't do anything, can they?"

And Dad said, "I wish you'd said that last night, then I might have been able to eat my egg while it was still hot."

"I wish Billy had said that last night as well," said Ray.

"Why?" said Dad.

"Then I wouldn't have had to listen to your awful singing, Dad."

Days

CHARLES CAUSLEY

Let it sleet on Sunday,
Monday let it snow,
Let the mist on Tuesday
From the salt-sea flow.
Let it hail on Wednesday,
Thursday let it rain,
Let the wind on Friday
Blow a hurricane,
But Saturday, Saturday
Break fair and fine
And all day Saturday
Let the sun shine.

The Birthday Cake

MARGARET MAHY

Molly was a girl with five aunts, and their names all began with the letter C . . . Cath, Connie, Carla, Clarissa and Caroline. But Molly never got them mixed up because Cath was tall and dark and rode to work on a bicycle, singing as she pedalled through the city, whereas Connie was little and fair and drove around town in a sports car. Carla was dark like Cath but she worked in the top of a tall building where she had a desk and a computer all to herself. Molly couldn't tell what colour Clarissa's hair really was because Clarissa dyed her hair red and wore it short and spiky, while Caroline, who was the youngest aunt of all, had brown hair hanging down in plaits because she was still going to school.

Of all the aunts, Caroline was the only one who stayed still. The others moved around, working first in the city and then in the country and then going back to the city again. But they all enjoyed being aunts and they never forgot Molly. When her birthday came around they all sent her presents and cards. Cath's presents were delicious ones like home-made fudge, whereas Connie sent pretty presents like bracelets hung with bells, and Carla liked clever presents... puzzles and magic tricks and packs of cards. Clarissa always chose funny presents... false noses and flowers that squirted water at you when you went to smell them, while Caroline always made Molly's presents herself... a cardboard tiger mask perhaps.

Molly's house was an ordinary house with all the usual things that houses have... things like washing machines and vacuum cleaners. However, Molly's mother and father were adventurous people and Molly was too. They went to lonely places in the summer weekends, and slept in tents and cooked over camp-fires. They had a lot of practice at living close to grass

and trees and sometimes close to wind and rain, and this was just as well because one day Molly's father went to work on an island... a small green island, pointed and lonely, where nobody lived except a few fishermen. His job was building a shed, and a new jetty so that the fishing boats could unload and Mr Cameron the delivery man could deliver mail and groceries to the island. Suddenly Molly's ordinary house was locked up and Molly and her mother went to live on the island too. They had no house to live in. Instead they lived in a caravan on the edge of the bush, and slept in bunks, not beds. Molly had the top bunk. They had no electricity so they had no washing machine or vacuum cleaner, and they cooked on the top of a little stove that ran on cylinders of gas. They could fry and boil and stew things but they couldn't bake. The oven did not work very well.

"Never mind!" said Molly's mother. "We won't cook oven things until we get home again."

In front of the caravan the sea stretched out until it ran into the sky. On grey days you couldn't tell where the sea stopped and the sky began. Molly's father and his helpers worked at one end of the beach building the jetty, and in the distance Molly and her mother could see other islands like floating grey-green ghosts.

Of course there was no school on the island but Molly's school work arrived in big green canvas envelopes sent by a correspondence school from somewhere in the middle of the city. Mr Cameron brought the envelopes out in his faithful boat *Sally*, zig-zagging from one island to another, leaving a ribbon of lacy foam and swelling ripples behind him. Molly and her mother knew *Sally* was due every second day (unless the weather was bad) and they would go down onto the old jetty to meet her.

Mr Cameron would shout to Molly's father, and then wink at Molly and say "How're you going, mate?" And then he would deliver not only the correspondence school lessons but letters from Molly's grandparents and from her five aunts, two dark ones, one fair, one redhead and one with brown plaits. All the aunts said how they missed Molly, and Caroline sent lots of pictures. Molly stuck them up one after another on the wall beside her caravan bunk.

"I like living on the island," said Molly, "but sometimes I miss our old house."

"We'll be home by Christmas," said Molly's mother.

Molly thought of Christmas . . . and then, all of a sudden, she thought of her birthday.

"What about my birthday?" asked Molly.

"Yes! An island birthday this year," her mother told her. "An island party too. No cake!"

"No cake!" cried Molly.

"Not this year. No oven," said her mother.

"But you have to have a cake to make it a birthday," Molly said. "A cake and presents and aunts."

"No you don't," said her mother, "All you need is a birthday girl."

"If there's no cake it won't be a proper birthday," Molly cried.

"Yes it will," said her mother. "We'll make up a new

sort of party, and you'll be the only one in the world to have a birthday like it."

Molly thought about a birthday with no birthday cake. Secretly she thought that a birthday without a birthday cake would be just another day, even if it was a particularly nice day. A cake with candles on it was the sign of a birthday and nothing else would be quite as birthdayish. She thought that that year she would have to do without a real birthday, and just pretend to have one.

The day of the birthday came, and it was a beautiful day. Molly's mother and father sang "Happy Birthday" very loudly and the waves broke softly on the shore saying, "Hush, hush!" Molly's parents gave her a lovely clown doll with big yellow shoes and a bobble on his hat all wrapped up in flowery paper but it still didn't quite feel like a proper birthday.

Trailing her white lace and her ripples, the good boat *Sally* came cutting through the waves with Mr Cameron looking out of the little cabin, even though it wasn't his day to deliver the mail. He waved to them, as he drew *Sally* up beside the beach. Then he paddled through the shallow water carrying his mail bag. Molly and her mother went to meet him. The mail bag looked as if it might be heavy.

"How about a cup of tea for a kind old man?" he said to Molly. "I had so many parcels here I thought I'd better make a special trip. The funny thing is all

these parcels are addressed to the same person."

"Who are they addressed to?" Molly asked.

"Molly McIntosh," said Mr Cameron. "Anyone of that name here?"

"Me!" said Molly. "It's my birthday."

"I thought it must be," said Mr Cameron.

Then he put his hand into his bag and brought out a big square parcel with a picture on it. The picture showed an enormous birthday cake.

"It's from Cath," said Molly's mother, but Molly was already opening her birthday present.

Under the paper was cardboard and under the cardboard was a tin with a tight-fitting lid.

Molly opened the tin. Inside was a wonderful birthday cake iced with white icing. There was a name iced on to the birthday cake. MOLLY it read.

"Mum!" cried Molly. "Look! A birthday cake after all."

"And a card," said her mother.

"Dear Molly," said the card. "I know you are out on the island without an oven, so it seems to me that you might need a birthday cake this birthday. It is particularly delicious because I have put cherries and nuts and raisins in it. Happy birthday!" The card was signed "Aunt Cath".

"Wonderful," said Mr Cameron! "But that's not all."

He took another big square parcel from the mail bag.

"Something from Connie," said Molly's mother, but

Molly was already opening her second present.

Under the paper was cardboard and inside the cardboard was a pretty blue tin with ducks on it. Molly opened the tin. Inside was a cake with pink icing and her name MOLLY iced on it in white. There were white sugar roses and chains of white beads. The cake had been so carefully packed that the white beads and roses were hardly broken at all. Another birthday cake.

"There's a card," said Molly's mother. Molly read the card.

"Dearest Molly. You are so far away this birthday. I know you don't have an oven so I have sent a birthday cake for you. I am not a wonderful cook like Cath but I have made the cake as *pretty* as I can. Your loving Aunt Connie."

"Two cakes," said Mr Cameron. "I've never had two cakes in my whole life, and I've had a lot more birthdays than you have. And, blow me down! Here's another present that looks rather like more of the same thing!" Another square parcel. More cardboard, another tin . . . this time a tin with roses on it. Another cake, from Aunt Carla this time. It was iced in white but this cake had the letter painted on it. "Dear Molly," said the letter. "I know you don't have an oven on the island so I thought I would send you a birthday cake and a birthday letter all in one. Your loving Aunt Carla. PS This letter is painted on with food colouring, so it is safe to eat it, full stops and all."

"A letter you can eat," said Mr Cameron. "That's clever."

"It's from Carla . . . and she *is* a clever aunt," agreed Molly. Mr Cameron passed her another present. This time it was a flat box tied up with red string. Molly pulled the string off and opened the box.

"It's a sort of balloon," said Molly's mother. "Blow it up and let's have a look at it."

Molly blew on the balloon. It was hard to blow up. Her cheeks puffed out and puffed out until they hurt, and then suddenly the balloon began to swell. It was a birthday cake balloon . . . its icing was painted green and yellow and it even had candles.

HAPPY BIRTHDAY it said in bright green icing. On the side of the balloon birthday cake was a smiling face. "Love from Clarissa," said a card slipped into the box beside the balloon cake.

"Four birthday cakes," said Molly. "I thought I wouldn't have one cake and I've got four."

"Some people have all the luck!" declared Mr Cameron. "Nothing left now, except this envelope." The envelope was a very big one. The address was written in seven different colours. It was more like a rainbow than an address.

MOLLY MCINTOSH,
SKIPPER'S ISLAND,
SKIPPER'S GULF,
NEW ZEALAND,
THE WORLD,
THE UNIVERSE,
SPACE.

"It's from Caroline," cried Molly.

Caroline had painted a picture of a birthday cake . . . a birthday cake that was bigger than a house. An elephant stood looking up at it admiringly.

"She's painted the biggest birthday cake in the world," Molly cried, "and it's mine. I'm going to put it up beside my bunk so that I can look at it at night."

Then Molly's father and his helpers took a break for afternoon tea, and Mr Cameron joined them and everyone had a slice of birthday cake and one and all agreed it was the best birthday cake they had ever tasted and said that that was probably the first time there had ever been a birthday on that particular island, and Molly stood looking at her five birthday cakes, thinking how strange it was to have a birthday that came over the sea towards her and how nice it was to have five birthday cakes . . . delicious, pretty, clever, funny, home-made birthday cakes on the day that she thought she would have no birthday cakes at all. But things like that can happen, even on an island, if you have the right sort of aunts.

Jamie

NAOMI LEWIS

Jamie collected white pebbles
In case he was in a wood.
For he'd read his Hansel and Gretel
As everybody should.

One day we went for a picnic
The day before he was six.
Jamie took the *Red Fairy Book*.
Kate took *The Secret Garden*,
And Tom took *Asterix*.

The common was pink with heather,
And springy to sit upon.
The trees grew tall at the border,
For there the forest began.

The wonderful smell of the forest
Mingled with our tea.
It smelled of bracken and toadstools
And damp leaves under the tree.

When we had finished the feasting
Everyone helped to clear
Everyone? Where was Jamie?
When did he disappear?

We searched. The daylight dwindled,
And dusk fell, like a hood,
Then suddenly we saw Jamie
Come smiling out of the wood.

"Yes, it was there," said Jamie,
"A little house made of cake
And sweets and things; but I didn't stay
In case the witch should wake.

I brought back the white pebbles
And some things for you," he said.
He held out some wild strawberries
And a piece of gingerbread.

A little house in the forest
Made of cake? Oh, that's absurd!
But *there* was the piece of gingerbread.

Nobody said a word.

When You Are Six

SHEILA LAVELLE

Emma had ten goldfish, seven rabbits, five hamsters, two tortoises, and a parrot that could sing God Save the Queen.

But Emma wanted a dog.

"Please, Mum," she said one morning at breakfast-time. "I would look after it. I would feed it and brush it and take it for walks, all by myself."

"No, Emma," said Mum, pouring cornflakes into a bowl. "You're only five years old. You're much too little to have a dog."

"Couldn't I just have a little dog?" said Emma.

Dad looked at Emma over the top of his newspaper.

"Stop pestering, Emma," he said. "You're too young to have a dog. I don't want to hear any more about it."

Emma poured milk over her cornflakes.

"When will I be old enough?" she asked.

"When you are six," said Mum.

Emma counted on her fingers. This was March, and her birthday was in June. That was three whole months from now. It seemed a long time to wait.

Then Emma had an idea. She ran upstairs and brought down a toy dog with pink ears and a curly tail.

"Look, Mum. Here's Muffin," she said. "He's a pretend dog. I can practise feeding him and brushing him and taking him for walks. Then when I get my real dog, I'll know how to look after it."

"That's very sensible of you, Emma," said Dad. He swallowed the last of his toast and marmalade and went out to dig the garden.

After breakfast, Mum and Emma and Muffin went to the library. While Mum was choosing her books, Emma looked on the shelf marked ANIMALS. She could read the word ANIMALS because she had an animal book at home.

She found books about elephants and chimpanzees, crocodiles and snakes, bears and kangaroos. But there was nothing about dogs, so she asked the librarian.

"You're looking in the wrong place," said the librarian. She showed Emma another shelf marked PETS.

Emma thought it was silly to have PETS and ANIMALS on different shelves. Pets were animals, weren't they? But she didn't bother to argue about it, for she could see just the sort of book she wanted.

The book was almost as big as Emma, but she heaved it down from the shelf and looked inside. There were pictures of dogs of all shapes and sizes. There were pictures of feeding bowls and dog baskets and brushes and combs and collars and leads and everything you needed to know about looking after a dog.

"What do you want that enormous thing for?" said Mum, as Emma carried the book to the counter to be stamped. "You can't even read."

"Yes I can," said Emma. "I can read my animal book at home."

Mum laughed. "Only because Dad has read it to you a hundred times," she said. "But you can look at the pictures, I suppose."

Emma was very busy for the next few weeks. Every day she looked at a new page in the big book, and every day she learnt something new about dogs. She saved her pocket money until she had enough to buy a brush and a comb, and she brushed Muffin until he was almost bald.

She stopped having sweets and crisps every time she went shopping with Mum, and Mum bought a tin of Woofy Chunks instead. Soon there was a big pile of tins in the larder, and Mum gave her an old soup plate to use as a feeding dish.

One Saturday, when Emma was out for a walk with Dad, she saw a notice on the door of the church hall.

"What does that say, Dad?" she asked.

"It says BOY SCOUTS' JUMBLE SALE," Dad told her.

"Can we go in?" said Emma.

"Why?" said Dad. "Do you want to buy a boy scout?"

"I want a second-hand basket for my dog," said Emma.

"You mean second-paw," said Dad, but he took Emma into the hall and helped her to find an almost-new basket for only fifty pence. Emma carried it home and put it on the floor in the kitchen.

"That's nice," said Mum. "All you need now is a blanket."

At school Emma was learning to knit. She asked her teacher to help her to knit a blanket for her dog's basket.

"What's that?" said Dad, when she brought it home.

"It's a blanket," said Emma. "I knitted it all by myself. It's for my dog."

Dad laughed. "I thought it was a fishing net," he said. "It's got so many holes."

He gave Emma a packet of seeds. "Here, you can plant those for your dog," he said.

Emma looked at the packet. There was a picture of a cauliflower on the front.

"Dogs don't eat cauliflowers," she said.

"Collie dogs might," said Dad.

Emma sighed. Grown-ups could be silly sometimes.

One morning Emma put a bit of string round Muffin's neck and took him for a walk down the path to the front gate.

"I don't think he wants to go for a walk," said the milkman.

"No," said Emma. "He keeps falling over. I expect it's because he hasn't got a proper collar and lead."

Next day when the milkman came he had a present for Emma. Emma opened it, and found a smart red lead and a brown leather collar.

"They're too small for my dog now," said the milkman. "Muffin can have them."

"Thank you," said Emma.

She put the collar and lead on Muffin. Muffin still fell over, but Emma didn't mind. Now she had everything she needed for her real dog, and there were only two more weeks to wait.

Emma's friend Katie was seven. She had a big black dog called Geordie, and every day after school she took him for a walk in the park. Every day Emma looked over the garden gate at Katie and Geordie going past.

"Can I come with you?" said Emma one afternoon. "I want to take my dog for a walk, too."

Katie looked at Muffin and laughed.

"You're not bringing that thing to the park," she said scornfully. "You can come with me when you've got a real dog." And she walked away.

Emma went to look at the calendar in the kitchen. Mum was there, making chips for tea.

"Only five more days," said Mum with a smile. "It's your birthday on Saturday." Emma danced round the kitchen. Five days wasn't very long at all.

Five days became four days, then three, then two, then one.

Then at last it was Saturday. Emma had lots of presents and cards. All of the cards had number six on them.

"NOW I am six!" said Emma.

Straight after breakfast Dad drove Emma to the Dogs' Home to choose her dog. There were big ones and little ones, fat ones and thin ones, smooth ones and furry ones. They were all so nice that Emma didn't know which one to choose.

In the end it was a black and white spaniel which chose Emma. He jumped up at her and wagged his tail like mad.

"I'll have this one," said Emma. "I'm going to call him Fred."

"Why?" said Dad.

"Because that's his name," said Emma.

As soon as she got home, Emma gave Fred a bowl of Woofy Chunks. She brushed and combed him until his coat shone. Then she put his collar and lead on him and opened the back door.

"Where are you going, Emma?" said Mum.

"I'm taking Fred for a walk," said Emma.

Dad looked at Emma over the top of his newspaper.

"Oh no you're not," he said. "You're much too young to take a dog out all by yourself."

Emma sighed as she looked out of the window at Katie going by with Geordie.

"When will I be old enough?" she said in a small voice.

"When you are seven," said Mum and Dad together.

MORE TITLES FROM
FRANCES LINCOLN CHILDREN'S BOOKS

Acker Backa Boo!

Opal Dunn

Illustrated by Susan Winter

Fantastic playground action rhymes from around the world,
collected by a specialist in early language development.

ISBN 978-1-84507-515-6

All the Colours of the Earth

Selected by Wendy Cooling

Illustrated by Sheila Moxley

The inspired voices of poets such as Benjamin Zephaniah,
Rabindranath Tagore and Margaret Mahy reflect cultures
from India to Australia, from the U.S.A. to Hungary,
and from China to the Caribbean.

ISBN 978-1-84507-101-1

Skip Across the Ocean
Nursery Rhymes from Around the World

Floella Benjamin

Illustrated by Sheila Moxley

All over the world, parents entertain and comfort children
with play rhymes and lullabies, and every country has its
own unique store of them. Floella Benjamin has selected
the best of these from six continents, some familiar,
some never before written down.

ISBN 978-1-84507-788-4

Frances Lincoln titles are available from all good bookshops.
You can also buy books and find out more about your favourite titles,
authors and illustrators on our website: www.franceslincoln.com